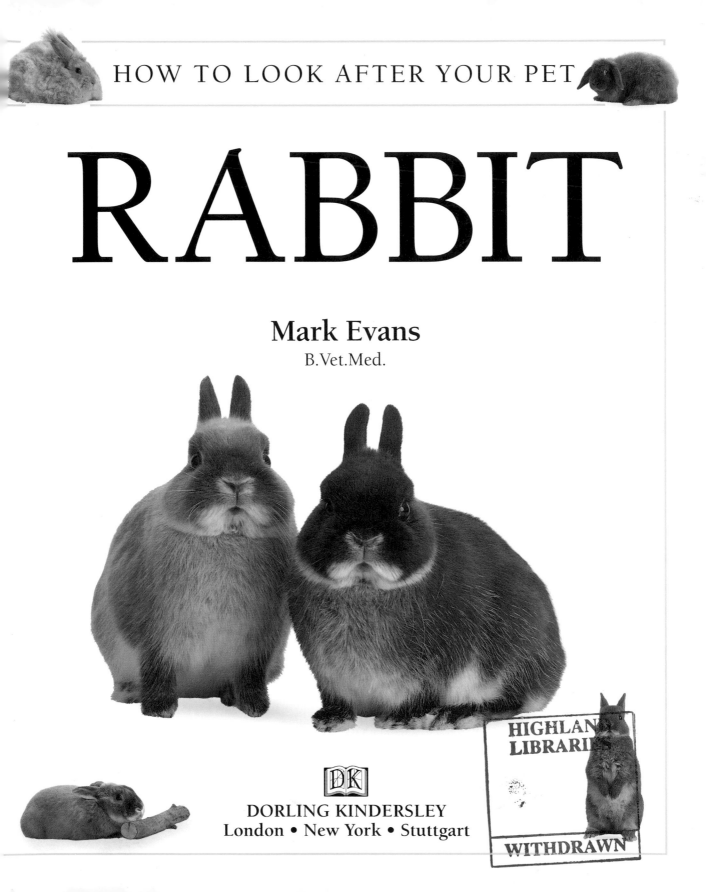

RABBIT

Mark Evans

B.Vet.Med.

DORLING KINDERSLEY

London • New York • Stuttgart

A DORLING KINDERSLEY BOOK

For Grandma

Project Editor Liza Bruml
Art Editor Jane Coney
Editor Miriam Farbey
Designer Rebecca Johns
Photographer Steve Shott
Illustrator Malcolm McGregor

First published in Great Britain in 1992 by
Dorling Kindersley Limited, 9 Henrietta Street,
London WC2E 8PS

A CIP catalogue record for this book
is available from the British Library.

ISBN 0-86318-903-2

Colour reproduction by Colourscan, Singapore
Printed and bound by Arnoldo Mondadori, Verona, Italy

Models: Stella Andreou, Jacob Brubert, Martin Cooles,
Minnie Copping, Laura Douglas, Simon Gangadeen,
Steven Gangadeen, Pete Hodson, Corinne Hogarth,
Thanh Huynh, Jason Kerim, Nathalie Lyon, Rachel Mamauag,
Paul Mitchell, Katie Murray, Florence Prowen, Isabel Prowen,
Edward Tillett, Lisa Wardropper

Dorling Kindersley would like to thank everyone who allowed
us to photograph their pet, Jane Burton, Pauline's Pets and Wood
Green Animal Shelters for providing rabbits, Oxford Scientific
Films Ltd, Christopher Howson for design help, SalvoTomasselli
for the world map and Lynn Bresler for the index.

Picture credits: Paul Bricknell p7 b, p8 tr, p9 b, c, p18 tl, p41 b,
p44 tl, b, back cover c; Philip Dowell p24 tr; Oxford Scientific
Films/Eyal Bartov p13 tr; Tim Shepherd p12 t, p12-13 c

Note to parents
This book teaches your child how to be a caring and responsible pet owner. But remember, your child must have your help and guidance in every aspect of day-to-day pet care. Don't let your child keep a rabbit unless you are sure that your family has the time and resources to look after it properly – for the whole of its life.

Contents

Introduction

The first step to becoming a good rabbit owner is to choose the right kind and size of rabbit, and a suitable hutch. Rabbits with short hair are the easiest to care for. If you get a large rabbit, you must have plenty of space for it to live in. Rabbits like to have company, but as they can fight with other rabbits, you will make the best friend for your pet. You'll need to look after your rabbit every day. Not just to start with, but for the whole of its life.

Shopping basket full of things you will need

Understanding your pet

You should try to get to know your rabbit well. If you handle it gently and talk to it as often as you can, it will quickly learn to trust you. Watch your pet carefully. You will soon begin to understand the fascinating sounds and other movements it makes to tell you things.

Rabbits' ears perk up to listen out for sounds

Caring for your pet

You will only be your pet's best friend if you care for it properly. You will need to make sure that it eats the right foods, always has water, and gets plenty of exercise every day. You will also have to groom it regularly, and keep its hutch clean.

You will need to brush your rabbit every day

Things to do with your pet
Your rabbit likes to keep busy. If you play with it every day, you will show everyone that you are a good pet owner.

Hand feed your rabbit so it learns to trust you

People to help
The best rabbit owner always tries to find out more about her pet. The vet and nurse at your local vet centre will check that your rabbit is healthy. You can ask them anything you like about how to keep your pet fit and happy.

You will need to visit your vet centre regularly

New family member
Your rabbit will be a very special part of your whole family. Everyone will want to stroke it, and be interested in what it does. Your rabbit can even become good friends with some of your other pets. You can also introduce it to your friends that like animals.

Ask a grown-up
👫 When you see this sign in the book, you should ask an adult to help you.

Your rabbit will become part of your family

Things to remember
When you live with a pet rabbit, there are some important rules you must always follow:

🐾 Wash your hands after stroking or playing with your pet, and after cleaning its hutch.

🐾 Don't kiss your rabbit.

🐾 Never give your rabbit food from your plate.

🐾 If your rabbit is hiding or in its bed, don't annoy it.

🐾 Never tease your rabbit.

🐾 Always watch your rabbit when it is with other pets.

🐾 Never, ever hit your rabbit.

9

What is a rabbit?

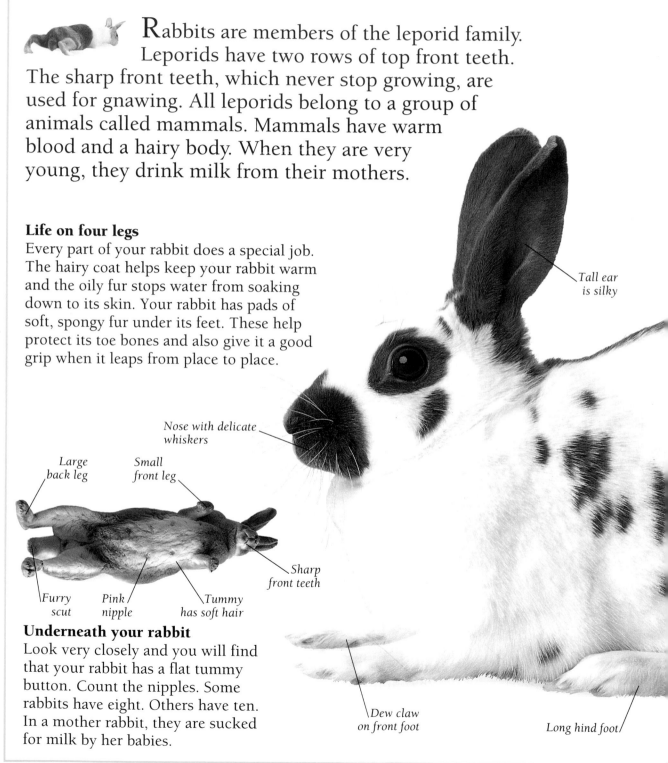

Rabbits are members of the leporid family. Leporids have two rows of top front teeth. The sharp front teeth, which never stop growing, are used for gnawing. All leporids belong to a group of animals called mammals. Mammals have warm blood and a hairy body. When they are very young, they drink milk from their mothers.

Life on four legs

Every part of your rabbit does a special job. The hairy coat helps keep your rabbit warm and the oily fur stops water from soaking down to its skin. Your rabbit has pads of soft, spongy fur under its feet. These help protect its toe bones and also give it a good grip when it leaps from place to place.

Tall ear is silky

Nose with delicate whiskers

Large back leg

Small front leg

Sharp front teeth

Furry scut

Pink nipple

Tummy has soft hair

Underneath your rabbit

Look very closely and you will find that your rabbit has a flat tummy button. Count the nipples. Some rabbits have eight. Others have ten. In a mother rabbit, they are sucked for milk by her babies.

Dew claw on front foot

Long hind foot

Ear stands tall

Long eyebrows are used to feel

Whiskers sense dangers around face

Nose sniffs the weakest of smells

Oily fur helps to keep rabbit dry

Large mouth has room for 28 teeth

Metal ring with rabbit's details

Small fluffy tail is called a scut

Always alert
Your rabbit has very keen senses. Its twitching nose picks up the faintest smells. Its large ears move in every direction to pick up sounds. It can see better than you in dim light.

Powerful back legs kick out

Long back straightens out

Front feet absorb shock

In full flight
Your rabbit moves fast in leaps and bounds. You can see your rabbit's big back legs when it is jumping. They are powered by strong muscles. Its short front legs help it to balance.

Look closer at your rabbit

The front teeth are very big. They gnaw tough food

Sharp nails on front paw are used for burrowing in soil

Four nails on back paw are good for scratching and grooming the coat

White scut is held up to warn other rabbits of danger

11

Life in the wild

Wild rabbits live together in groups in a warren. A warren has underground rooms, called burrows, which are dug by the females. The burrows are linked by narrow tunnels. Some of the burrows are used for sleeping. Others, called stops, are lined with fur to make nests for the babies. All the female rabbits in the warren are ruled by a female leader.

Warren door wide enough for one rabbit

Rabbit grazes on grass outside

Long tunnel leads down to nest room

Rabbit stays close to home in case of danger

Wild rabbit has grey, speckled coat

Mother rabbit in the nest she has dug for her young

Nest lined with grass and fur

Life in the warren

Female rabbits make the warren by burrowing. They dig with their front paws, and kick the soil away with their strong back legs. Rabbits sleep in their warren during the day, and graze at dawn and dusk, when their enemies can't see them.

Brave male sits on top of the warren, watching for danger

Young rabbit gnaws at root

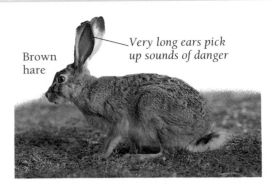

Brown hare

Very long ears pick up sounds of danger

Big ears!

Rabbits and hares seem to look the same. But hares have bigger ears, and their longer legs help them run faster than rabbits. Hares don't dig warrens to live in. They live alone in shallow holes, called forms, that they scrape in the ground.

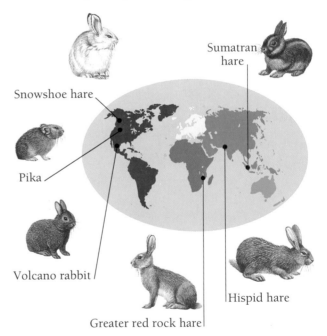

Sumatran hare

Snowshoe hare

Pika

Volcano rabbit

Greater red rock hare

Hispid hare

A worldwide family

Pet rabbits belong to the leporid family. All leporids are members of a group of animals called lagomorphs. The group includes many different kinds of rabbits, hares and pikas. Lagomorphs live in many parts of the world.

All shapes and sizes

A long time ago, French monks kept wild rabbits for food in walled gardens. They noticed that some rabbits were born with different features – long, shaggy coats, or patterned fur. By choosing which rabbits had babies, the monks began to make different types, or breeds.

Very small, pointed ear

Netherland Dwarf

Long ear has black tip

Belgian Hare

English Lop

Droopy or perked ears

Most types of rabbit have upright ears. These ears can be tall or short. Sometimes they are nearly as big as a hare's ears. Other types of rabbit have large, floppy ears that can touch the ground. They can't hear as well as those rabbits with upright ears.

Flat nose

Wide head

German Lop

Narrow head

Long and thin nose

Tan

Face shapes

A rabbit's head can be narrow and pointed, or broad and flat. Male rabbits have slightly wider heads than their sisters. The faces of some "lop" breeds of rabbit are so flat that they look as if they have been squashed.

Small, medium, large

Wild rabbits are all about the same size. Pet rabbits can be tiny, or very large. The smallest may be called dwarfs or minis. Some huge types are called giants. Find out how big the rabbit that you like the look of will grow.

Medium-sized, slim rabbit

Large ears on "mini" rabbit

Small rabbit has dark ears

Largest breed of rabbit

Himalayan

Mini-rex

English Lop

Flemish Giant

Coat is shiny

Thick fur feels plush

Soft, short coat is waterproof

Normal fur

Satin

Rex

How a rabbit gets its looks

Two rabbits of the same breed have an identical child

The child looks the same as its parents

Very long, silky hair

Types of fur

There are several kinds of rabbit coat. Some rabbits have soft fur called satin. Others have velvety fur called rex. Angora and Cashmere rabbits have long, fine hair that tangles easily. They can't keep it tidy themselves, so they need to be brushed very regularly.

Long hair is fluffy

Cashmere

Angora

Two different breeds of rabbit will produce a mix, or crossbred

The child looks a little like both of its parents

New Zealand White

Pure white fur

Colourful coats

Wild rabbits have speckled fur, called agouti. Pet rabbits may have agouti fur, or their fur may be all one colour, such as white, black, grey or chocolate. Some pet rabbits have patterned coats of two or more colours. They can have patches, spots and stripes.

Brown and orange fur

Two crossbred rabbits can have almost anything

Brown face

The offspring is a real mixture

White chest

Tri-coloured Dutch

White collar

Bi-coloured French Lop

Your rabbit's home

Before you go to collect your rabbit, you must get it a hutch to live in. Rabbits are very active, so the hutch must have plenty of space. Put the hutch in a sheltered place, where it is safe from any other animals. Remember to stock up with rabbit food (see p24). You will also need to buy bedding, litter and feeding equipment.

Roof overhangs to protect from rain

Roof slopes so that rain runs off

Bedroom for sleeping and hiding away

Solid door helps keep room warm

Measure the size of the hutch

Apple tree branch

Sheets of paper
You need some large pieces of paper to line the floor of the hutch. Old drawing paper or newspaper is ideal.

Lining the hutch
Buy wood shavings to put on the hutch floor. These soak up urine. Buy straw for your rabbit to make its bed in. Get some fresh, dry hay for your rabbit to eat.

Wood shavings

Hay

Straw

Hay rack
Buy a hay rack to fix to the hutch door. Your rabbit can pull hay from it to eat. The hay will be kept clean in the rack as your pet cannot trample it.

Gnawing log
Find a small tree branch for your rabbit to gnaw on. Gnawing helps to keep the teeth healthy. A branch from a fruit tree is best.

Wire mesh lets in fresh air

Roof felt keeps hutch waterproof

60 cm

The hutch should be 120 cm wide and 60 cm deep

Long legs lift the hutch off wet ground and out of reach of animal enemies

80 cm

Bowl
Buy a large food bowl. It must not be plastic as your rabbit may gnaw it.

Pottery bowl is hard to tip

Food container
You need a container in which to store your rabbit's food.

Airtight box keeps food fresh

Water bottle
Buy a water bottle with a dropper. The dropper lets out water when your rabbit sucks the end of the metal tube.

Metal dropper

Mineral lick
Rabbits need to eat plenty of mineral salts. Buy a special salt lick.

Where to put the hutch

Make sure cats and other animals can't get into the hutch

Keep the rabbit hutch shaded from bright sunshine

Shelter the rabbit hutch from wind and rain

Your rabbit will freeze if left out in the bitter cold

Put the hutch in a place where you can look at it often

The hutch
👭 Look at the measurements in the picture. This hutch is just large enough for a small rabbit. If you get two rabbits or a large rabbit, the hutch should be bigger. All hutches must have two rooms. The large room is a living room, the small room is a bedroom.

Indoor cage
You can keep your rabbit indoors. It needs a small cage to sleep in. The cage must be big enough for your rabbit to stretch out in when it is lying down on its side.

Things to get ready

You will need to get some special equipment to help you look after your new pet. It does not need to be expensive, but it should be well made, as rabbits chew everything they find. Make sure the equipment is ready before you bring your rabbit home.

Holes let in air for rabbit to breathe

Carrying box
Ask your vet for a special box in which to carry your rabbit.

Old tray

Sliding pin keeps lid firmly closed

Wire basket
You can get a strong wire cage to carry your rabbit in. It will last longer than the carrying box.

Weighing scales
You will need to weigh your rabbit to check that it is healthy. Find old kitchen scales to weigh a young or small rabbit. Weigh a larger rabbit on bathroom scales.

Rounded prongs won't scratch your rabbit

Brush   Comb

Grooming equipment
Your rabbit's hair will become tangled. Buy a small, soft brush and a fine comb to keep it clean and tidy.

Tightly fitting lid keeps litter fresh

Plastic bin

Scoop

Litter tray liners

Indoor rabbit equipment
If you keep your rabbit indoors, it will toilet in a litter tray. Buy a storage bin for the litter, plastic litter tray liners, and a scoop to fill and empty the tray.

Litter tray

Clay Straw Wood chips Garden earth

Litter tray and litter

A cat litter tray is just the right size for an indoor rabbit to use. Try different kinds of litter to see which your rabbit prefers.

Grazing ark

🏃 Buy or make a grazing ark so that your rabbit can run around and graze outside. The ark must have a covered area so your rabbit can shelter from the sun or hide if it is scared.

Wooden slat Wire mesh

Detergent

Disinfectant

Bucket

Scrubbing brush Dustpan Dustpan brush

Scraper

Rubber gloves

Bottle brush Spout brush

Cleaning equipment

To clean your rabbit's hutch, you will need some special things. Never take things that are used to clean your house. Ask your vet what type of disinfectant spray to buy. Keep all the cleaning equipment together, so it is not used to clean anything else.

Choosing your rabbit

You can choose a baby rabbit from a litter when it is six weeks old. The babies look so cuddly that you may want to take them all home. Only get more than one rabbit if you have a very big hutch (see p17). If you have room for two, it is best to choose baby females, as two males may fight.

Young kitten   Beautiful adult

Big or small?

Find out how big the type of rabbit that you want will grow. Some types of rabbits can become very large and need to live in a big hutch.

Baby or adult?
It is easy to fall in love with a tiny baby rabbit. A young rabbit is called a kitten. But remember, a kitten will soon grow up. An adult rabbit may be just as adorable.

Where to buy your rabbit
- A friend's rabbit may have babies.
- A breeder will have breed rabbits.
- An animal shelter may have all kinds of rabbits that need homes.

1 **When you go to choose** a baby rabbit, watch the litter with the owner from outside the enclosure. Try to spot the most playful kitten. Don't disturb the kittens.

Point to show the owner the kitten that you like

Owner watches her rabbits carefully

Kitten looks around curiously

Bold kitten sniffs the soil

2 Ask the owner to pick up the kitten that you think is the liveliest. Ask whether it is a male or a female. Remember, if you want to keep two rabbits, choose females. Check that the kitten hasn't been chosen by anyone else.

Hungry mother nibbles at carrot

Owner sits to hold your favourite kitten

3 The owner will let you hold the kitten. Make sure you are sitting down. Put the kitten on your lap so it feels safe. It should be very friendly. Now you can decide if you really like it.

Mother rabbit listens out for noises

Slowly stroke the kitten's ears

One hand keeps the kitten steady

4 Check that the rabbit is healthy. Ask the owner to show you how to pick it up. The rabbit should have bright eyes, and a clean nose and ears. The fur should be soft and dry all over. Remember to check the hidden places, like under the scut.

Cradle rabbit on its back to check the fur on its tummy

Carrying box to put your rabbit in on the journey home

Stay sitting down to do the health checks

Welcome home

Your new rabbit may be frightened when it first leaves its mother. You must have the hutch ready so that your new pet will settle down quickly. Cover the floor with paper and shavings. Put lots of straw in the bedroom and some in the living room. Fill the hay rack, food bowls and water bottle. Don't forget a gnawing log.

Vet listens to rabbit's heart through his stethoscope

Visiting your vet

Arrange to visit your vet on the way home from collecting your new rabbit. He will examine it all over to make sure it is healthy. Your vet will answer any questions you have about your new pet.

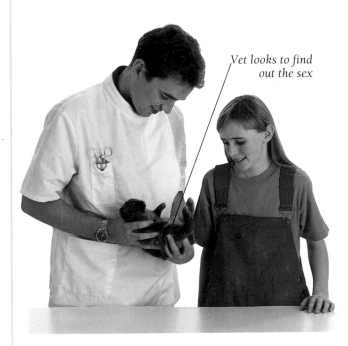

Vet looks to find out the sex

Checking the sex

When a rabbit is very young, it can be hard to tell if it is a male or a female. Ask your vet to check the sex of your rabbit, so you are sure it is the sex you wanted.

Male rabbit

Female rabbit

Male and female

The two pictures above will help you find out the sex of your pet. Look between its back legs.

Attach water bottle to door

Fix salt lick to wire mesh door

Spread wood shavings on the floor

Picking up your pet

Small rabbits are easier to pick up than large ones (see p31). To pick up a small rabbit, put one hand over its neck, and the other hand under its bottom. Scoop it up.

Be careful not to pull the ears

Hold your rabbit close to your chest

When to handle your new rabbit

Day 1: Put your rabbit in its hutch. Watch it, but don't disturb it.

Day 2: Your rabbit may hide in its bed. Talk to it, so it gets used to your voice.

Days 3 to 5: Offer your rabbit food from your hand. Stroke it, and try to pick it up.

Days 6 to 14: Stroke and brush your rabbit. Introduce it to your other pets (see p35).

After 2 weeks: Play with your rabbit every day. Let your rabbit out in its enclosure and grazing ark.

Your rabbit's new home

Carefully lift your rabbit out of its carrying box and into its hutch. Lock the doors, and leave it to explore its new home. Come back often to check your rabbit is settling down.

Fill hay rack with fresh hay

Put some straw in the living room

Bolt to keep the door firmly closed

Feeding your rabbit

 Rabbits are herbivores, which means they only eat plants. In the wild, they graze on seeds, roots and wild grasses. To keep your rabbit fit, you must feed it the same kind of food. You should give it specially prepared rabbit food. You can also take your rabbit out of its hutch to graze on grass (see p38).

Razor-sharp teeth bite off portions of food

Side teeth grind food

Mouth made for chewing
The food your rabbit eats needs to be very well chewed. A rabbit's teeth and mouth are specially made for biting and grinding. Food is mixed with spit in the mouth while it is ground by the teeth.

Grazing all day
Grass and some wild plants are favourite foods for rabbits. They have to eat a lot of greens to get enough goodness. Given the chance, your rabbit will spend many hours nibbling every day.

Dried food

Special foods
Even if your rabbit grazes on grass, you need to give it other food. It loves hay, which is dried grass. You must also buy your rabbit special food made from mixtures of dried plants, seeds and vegetables.

Hay is kept clean and tidy in the rack

Hay

Your rabbit spends a lot of time eating

When to feed your rabbit
Feed your rabbit every morning and evening. It must always have dried food to eat. Your rabbit won't make a store of food, like a squirrel or a hamster does.

Eating droppings

Do not worry if you see your rabbit eating its own droppings – all rabbits do this. Your rabbit's stomach can't take all the goodness from food the first time it eats it. So your pet makes soft droppings, which it eats again straight away.

Tip of tube has a little ball in it that stops water dripping

Fresh water

Wild rabbits get water from the fresh food they eat. Your rabbit eats a lot of dried food, so you must make sure that its water bottle is always full.

Screw lid on tightly

Fresh water

Pour new food into the bowl every morning and evening

An apple tree log is best

Grinding down teeth

Your rabbit's teeth grow all the time. Wild rabbits eat hard food, which wears down their teeth. Give your rabbit a log to gnaw. This will stop its teeth from growing too long.

How much to feed your rabbit

Each time you feed your rabbit, fill its bowl to the brim. Your rabbit should only eat as much food as it needs. If it has plenty of exercise, it won't get fat.

25

Feeding fresh foods

Vegetables and fresh fruit are full of goodness. You can give your rabbit spare vegetables, greens and fruit from your kitchen. You can also collect wild plants. But be careful! Some weeds are poisonous. Only feed a handful of fresh food every day, as too much will give your pet a tummy ache.

Wild plant food
These weeds are all safe to feed to your rabbit. Try to gather a handful of wild plants every other day. You can also let your rabbit graze on fresh grass (see p38).

Shepherd's purse

Chickweed

Dandelion

Clover

Hiding food
Finding food is a good game for your rabbit. A heap of hay or a pile of soil makes a perfect hiding place. Your rabbit can smell fresh food, and is expert at rooting it out.

Plantain

Heap of soil for digging in

♫ Food must be fresh
Fresh plants, fruit and vegetables quickly become stale. Throw away these foods if they haven't been eaten by bedtime. Never give your rabbit grass cuttings because they go mouldy very quickly.

26

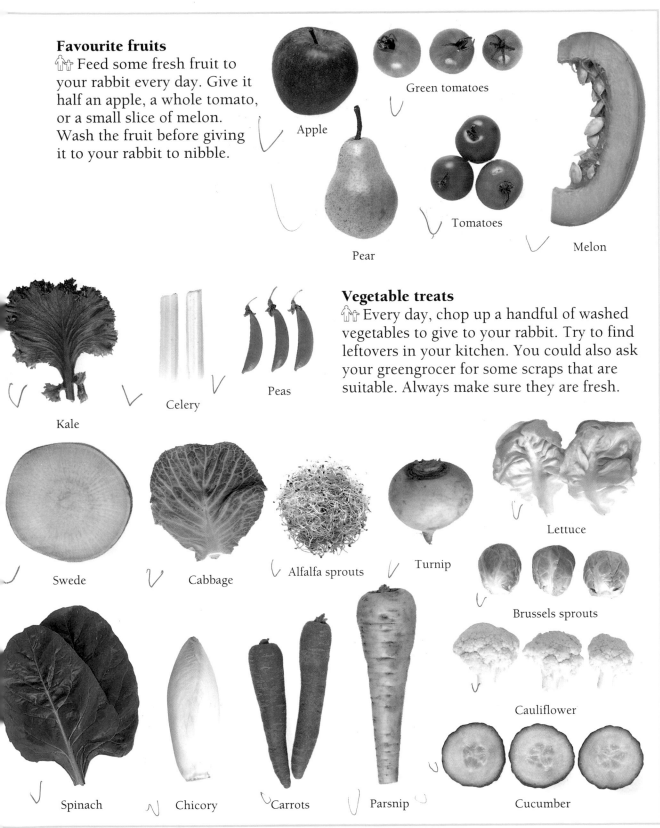

Favourite fruits

👥 Feed some fresh fruit to your rabbit every day. Give it half an apple, a whole tomato, or a small slice of melon. Wash the fruit before giving it to your rabbit to nibble.

Green tomatoes

Apple

Pear

Tomatoes

Melon

Vegetable treats

👥 Every day, chop up a handful of washed vegetables to give to your rabbit. Try to find leftovers in your kitchen. You could also ask your greengrocer for some scraps that are suitable. Always make sure they are fresh.

Kale

Celery

Peas

Swede

Cabbage

Alfalfa sprouts

Turnip

Lettuce

Brussels sprouts

Cauliflower

Spinach

Chicory

Carrots

Parsnip

Cucumber

27

Cleaning the hutch

Your rabbit likes its home to be very clean. If the hutch becomes dirty, it will start to smell and your rabbit will become ill. You should clean out the hutch and wash the feeding equipment every day. When you have finished, put down new paper and fresh straw, shavings and hay. Make sure the food bowl, hay rack and water bottle are full. Once a week, scrub out the hutch thoroughly.

1 **Every day, put your rabbit** in its carrying box. This will keep it safely out of the way while you clean the hutch. On a dry day, let your rabbit outside in its enclosure or grazing ark. Don't forget to take the rack, bowl and water bottle out of the hutch for cleaning.

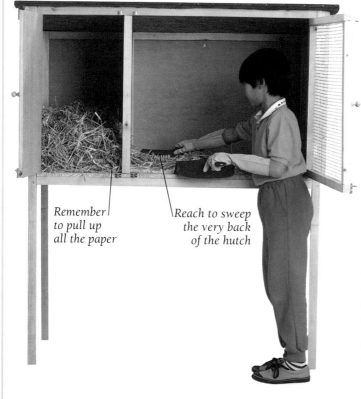

Remember to pull up all the paper

Reach to sweep the very back of the hutch

2 **Use your dustpan and brush** to sweep up the old straw, wood shavings, droppings and stale food. Wear the rubber gloves to keep your hands clean. Lift up all the lining paper. Throw away everything into a dustbin.

Don't scrape too hard, or you will damage the wood

3 Use your scraper to lift off any bits that are stuck to the floor or sides of the hutch. The corners will be dirtiest. Sweep up with the dustpan and brush.

Spray to kill germs *Scrub hard*

Bucket of hot, soapy water

Thorough clean
Once a week, use a brush and hot, soapy water to scrub the inside of the hutch. Rinse the hutch and then spray it with disinfectant. Leave it to dry out.

Washing the bowl
Wipe out the food bowl with the cloth. Soak it first if it is dirty. Dry it with a paper towel.

Wipe the cleaning cloth all around the bowl

Emptying the rack
Remove any uneaten hay from the hay rack. Don't throw the hay away. You can use it as bedding. Pack the rack with fresh hay for your rabbit to eat.

Clear drinking tube
Make sure nothing is blocking the bottle dropper. Brush the tube with the spout brush. Then shake the tube. You should hear the ball move.

Twist the brush inside the tube

Turn the brush to clean the sides

Clean water bottle
Pour hot, soapy water into the bottle. Scrub inside with the bottle brush. Rinse the bottle before filling it with cold, fresh water.

Good grooming

Your rabbit gets dirt and straw stuck in its coat. In spring, thick winter fur starts to loosen and fall out. This is called moulting. To keep itself tidy, your rabbit grooms itself. You can help your pet stay neat by brushing it every day. Brushing also helps it get used to being handled. If you have a Cashmere or an Angora, grooming untangles the long hair.

Paws are covered in spit, like soap, to clean face

Licked clean
A rabbit spends a lot of time grooming itself. It uses its front teeth as a comb to pick out dirt, and its tongue as a flannel. It wipes its face with its front paws.

Don't forget the fur on the tips of the Angora's ears

Brush one section of the fur at a time

Brushing short hair
To groom a short-haired rabbit, brush the hair on its back away from its head. Next brush its tummy and under its chin. Then comb all the parts in the same order.

Rosette for the owner of prize-winning rabbit

Grooming a long-hair
The hair of a Cashmere or Angora gets so tangled that it must be groomed a little bit at a time. Choose a part of the coat. Brush the hair, then comb it, then brush it again. Then choose another part.

Brush the back from the head to the tail

Best-cared-for rabbit wins prize

Picking up a large rabbit

Kneel down next to your pet

1 **Before picking up** a large rabbit, spread out a towel on the floor next to your pet. Sit down beside the towel. Gently push your rabbit onto the towel.

Stroke and cuddle your rabbit, so that it feels very safe

Lay large towel flat on floor

Rabbit sits facing your knees

Tuck every part of the towel close to the body

Keep stroking your rabbit's back so it feels safe

Use your weaker arm to support your pet's tummy

Use your stronger arm to support your pet's bottom

2 **Fold both sides of the towel** over your rabbit's back. Make sure every part of its body is covered except for its face and ears. Your rabbit will feel secure when it is wrapped up. It will not be able to wriggle when you pick it up.

3 **Lift your rabbit off the floor.** Put one hand under its bottom and the other under its tummy. When you have scooped your pet up, hold it close to your chest. Stand up only when you are sure that your rabbit is comfortable.

Understanding your rabbit

Your rabbit makes soft grunts, but these won't tell you its mood. You will know when your rabbit is terrified as it squeals. It also warns other rabbits of danger by thumping its back legs. A rabbit finds out a lot by sniffing. It can even tell from another rabbit's smell whether it is a friend or enemy. Watch your rabbit, and you will soon understand what it is doing.

Eye is nearly closed

Cuddling together
Rabbit kittens are very friendly. The brothers and sisters huddle together in a heap when they are sleeping. This helps to keep them warm.

Rabbit nuzzles its friend's chin

Marking what's mine
Your rabbit rubs special scent, which is made in its skin, onto everything in the hutch, grazing ark and enclosure. If your rabbit lives with another rabbit, it rubs its friend's chin to leave the scent.

Ears perk up to listen

Eye searches for danger

Keeping a lookout
When your rabbit hears a strange sound, it stands up on its hind legs to see what is happening.

Standing up allows rabbit to see farther

Best of friends
Your rabbit will show you that you are its friend. It rubs its head against you to leave its special scent. It may even wash you with its tongue!

Friendly rabbit licks your fingers

Rabbit sits happily on your lap

Signalling danger

When a mother rabbit thinks that her kittens are in danger, she will stand in front of them. If she is very worried, she will thump the ground with her back leg. This tells the kittens, and other nearby rabbits, to run for cover.

Mother rabbit shelters babies behind her

Back leg slams onto the ground

Timid rabbit twists head away in fear

Bossy rabbit glares at enemy

Meeting the enemy

A rabbit may become angry with another rabbit. It will stare straight at its enemy to show that it is annoyed.

Show of strength

If the timid rabbit doesn't run away, both rabbits will scratch the ground with their front paws. They may run at each other.

Head turns to avoid bite

Teeth grab enemy's neck

Claws scrape the ground

The fight

If neither rabbit is scared away, a fight begins. They charge forwards and try to sink their teeth into each other's necks.

Back leg may kick out

The loser

The weaker rabbit runs away when it is beaten. It will never forget the other rabbit's scent. Whenever it smells the other rabbit's scent, it will run off.

Friends for your pet

Your rabbit will get very lonely without any friends. In the wild, rabbits live in groups in a large warren. When two rabbits are kept together in a small hutch, they may fight. Unless you have a hutch that is large enough for two rabbits, you make the best friend for your pet.

Sisters are best!
You can keep two rabbits together if they are females. Two sisters from the same litter will get on best. You must have a very big hutch and a large enclosure.

Male rabbit does not help look after babies

The rabbit family
Do not keep a male and a female rabbit together unless you want them to have babies. Male and female rabbits kept in the same hutch will fight most of the time.

Babies suck milk from their mother's nipples

A rabbit each
If your brother or sister gets a rabbit, keep it in a separate hutch, unless both rabbits are baby females. You need to spend a lot of time with your rabbit to stop it being lonely.

You can be your rabbit's best friend

Stroke fur along back towards tail

Your rabbit sits happily while you stroke it

Be ready to pick your rabbit up if it is frightened

Rabbit sniffs the dog curiously

Rabbit sits very still

Bird friend
A small pet bird, such as a budgerigar, can make good friends with your rabbit. Your rabbit knows that the tiny bird is too small to harm it.

Meeting a dog
You can introduce your rabbit to a well-behaved dog, but never leave them alone together. Do not let your cat and rabbit meet. Your cat will attack your rabbit and frighten it.

Gently stroke the dog to keep him calm

Hold the lead firmly

Leaving your pet

Going on holiday
You can't always take your rabbit with you when you go on holiday. You must find someone to look after it. You may have a friend with a rabbit who has time to look after yours as well.

Making a check list
Make a list of the jobs that need doing every day, in the order that you do them. Your rabbit is used to this order and may be upset if it is changed. Note the name and telephone number of your vet.

What to pack
Get everything ready for your friend. Make sure you pack enough food, bedding and litter to last until you get back. Don't forget all the cleaning and grooming equipment.

Moving your rabbit
Take your rabbit to your friend in its carrying box, wire basket or small, indoor cage. Bring your grazing ark with you if your friend has nowhere for your pet to exercise.

The indoor rabbit

You can keep your rabbit indoors if you don't have a garden. Your rabbit will need a special cage to sleep in and a litter tray in which to go to the toilet. Your rabbit should spend most of the day out of its cage. Only keep two rabbits indoors if they are friends (see p34). They must have a cage each to sleep in. If you have other pets, beware – they may not want to be friends with your rabbit.

Toilet training your pet

You must train your rabbit to go to the toilet in its litter tray, or it will make a mess. Put it in the tray every few minutes. Your rabbit will soon learn to go to the tray by itself.

Cover the bottom of the tray with litter

Plastic liner

Rabbit sniffs sofa curiously

Naughty rabbit!

Your rabbit may try to chew and scratch the things in your home. If you spot your rabbit being naughty, say "No" in a loud voice. If your pet doesn't stop, spray it with some water.

Point firmly at your rabbit

Rabbit tries to chew leaves

Small cage for one rabbit to sleep in

The indoor cage

Your rabbit will sleep overnight in a cage. Get the biggest cage that you can. Cover the base with a layer of paper, wood shavings and straw. Put the cage in a safe corner, away from other pets. You must empty and clean it every day.

Carefully put your rabbit into its cage

Attach a water bottle filled with fresh water

Hay for your rabbit to eat

Make sure wires are out of reach of your rabbit

Dangers in the home

Keep electric wires out of reach of your pet

Sharp objects may cut your pet

Some dogs may harm your rabbit (see p35)

Hot drinks may spill and burn your rabbit

Keep doors closed so your pet can't escape

Be careful that no-one treads on your pet

Keeping busy

Your rabbit is very active. Playing around your house helps to keep it fit. You should let it out of the cage as much as possible. Always watch your rabbit to make sure that it is safe and does not damage anything in your house.

Litter tray filled with litter

Large bowl of water

Dried food in bowl

Paper keeps floor clean

Stroke your rabbit so it gets used to your touch

Rabbit looks for the next place to explore

The outdoor rabbit

Your rabbit loves to be outside. Ask an adult to help you make a corner of your garden into an enclosure. Make sure the wire fencing is buried into the ground or your rabbit may be able to burrow its way out of the enclosure. Stand the hutch in one corner, and put things in the area for your rabbit to play with. You should let your rabbit out of its hutch every day to exercise and graze.

Eating fresh grass
You can use the lid from an indoor rabbit's cage as a small grazing ark. Your rabbit will quickly nibble the patch of grass, so move the lid often. Always watch your rabbit when it is outside.

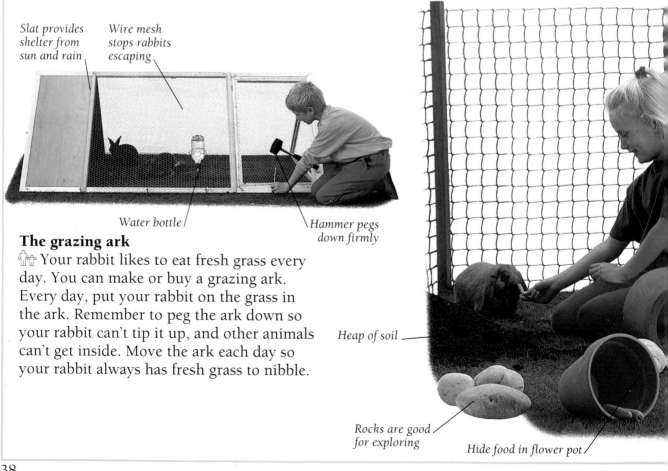

Slat provides shelter from sun and rain

Wire mesh stops rabbits escaping

Water bottle

Hammer pegs down firmly

The grazing ark
🧍🧍 Your rabbit likes to eat fresh grass every day. You can make or buy a grazing ark. Every day, put your rabbit on the grass in the ark. Remember to peg the ark down so your rabbit can't tip it up, and other animals can't get inside. Move the ark each day so your rabbit always has fresh grass to nibble.

Heap of soil

Rocks are good for exploring

Hide food in flower pot

The rabbit enclosure

It is fun to watch your rabbit play in its enclosure. If you have two rabbits, they may each need a hutch inside the enclosure (see p17). When you are not watching your rabbit, cover the area with wire mesh to stop any other animals from getting in.

Beware of these dangers

Prowling cats may jump into the area

Birds of prey may swoop down

Weedkillers on grass are poisonous

Dogs may scare your rabbit

Some plants will poison your pet

Shelter the area from bad weather and bright sun

Wire fence surrounds enclosure

Wire mesh lets fresh air in and keeps danger out

Plastic sheet to cover area when it rains

Ramp for rabbits to climb down

Fresh grass to nibble

Feed your rabbit by hand

Having babies

Just as a grown-up woman may have children, a female rabbit can have baby rabbits. These are called kittens. Think very carefully before keeping female and male rabbits together to breed. You will have to find good homes for all of the kittens. There may be as many as eight in a litter. Your vet may be able to give your rabbit a neutering operation. This stops it having babies.

♫ Responsible owner

It may seem like fun to let your female rabbit have kittens. But don't forget that these cuddly balls of fluff soon grow up. You will need to find each of them a new home.

Eye closed

Fur has begun to grow

Four-day-old kitten

1 **When a kitten is born** it can't see or hear. It has a keen sense of smell, so it can find its mother for a drink of milk. After four days, its fur starts to grow.

2 **Two-week-old kittens drink milk** from their mother. The milk gives them all the goodness they need to grow. The mother usually only lets the kittens drink once a day for about five minutes. Then she leaves them alone in the nest she has built for them.

Eye open so kitten can see

Kitten hears through long ear

Mother keeps a lookout

Kitten burrows in for a drink

Playful kitten climbs on top

Kitten cuddles up to keep warm

Kitten sniffs for scents

3 **At five weeks old**, the kittens have left their mother. They can eat solid food. They play with their brothers and sisters. When they are tired, they huddle together to keep warm. They will soon be ready to go to new homes.

4 **When a rabbit is five months old**, it looks like a small grown-up. Both male and female rabbits are now ready to have a family of their own. Keep them apart, unless you want your rabbits to breed.

Fur is thick and sleek

5 **As a rabbit grows older**, its body grows plumper and its back legs grow stronger. It needs to have a friend. You can become its best friend. You can keep it with another rabbit in a very large hutch (see p17).

Stroke your rabbit to show that you are its friend

Powerful back leg

Health care

You need to look after your rabbit properly to make sure it stays healthy. You should give it the right food (see p24), keep it well groomed (see p30), and make sure that it has plenty of room to exercise. You also need to do some simple health checks with your rabbit every day. You will learn to spot quickly if your pet is unwell. If you think something is wrong, take it to your vet.

Push the fur backwards

1 **Check your rabbit's coat** is in good condition. You can do this when you groom your pet. Push the fur backwards so you can see down to the skin. The fur should feel soft, and smell clean. Don't forget to look at the tummy and under the scut.

Carefully pull back the ear flap

2 **Examine your rabbit's ears.** Hold the ear very gently between your fingers. Look down the dark hole. The ear should be clean. If it smells, your rabbit could be ill.

3 **Look at your rabbit's eyes.** A bright light will help you see them better. The eyelids should be wide open. Each eye should be clear and shiny, with no tears in the corners.

Put your thumb above the eye

4 👥 Check your rabbit's front teeth. They must be straight, clean and bright white. If you think they may be too long, visit your vet.

Carefully push back the lips to look at the teeth

Gently hold the ears flat against the back to stop your rabbit wriggling

5 Pick up and check each paw in turn. Look carefully between the toes and underneath at the furry pads. Make sure nothing is stuck in the hair. Don't forget to check that the toenails are the right length.

Toenail is too long

Toenail is right length

Grip the paw between your thumb and fingers

Weighing your rabbit

Weigh your rabbit at the same time, on the same day, every week. Write down the weight. Wash the weighing tray thoroughly afterwards. If your rabbit has lost or gained weight, it may be ill, or it may not be getting enough exercise.

Line the tray with paper

Old scales

Your pet care check list

Use this list to keep a record of all the jobs you need to do.

Copy this chart. Tick off the jobs when you have finished them.

Every day:
Feed your rabbit
Fill the hay rack
Wash and fill bottle
Clean the bowls
Change the bedding
Put down new paper and wood shavings
Groom your rabbit
Look at coat
Check eyes and ears
Check teeth
Examine toenails
Put out to graze

◆

Once a week:
Scrub the hutch
Weigh your rabbit
Tidy the enclosure

◆

Every six months:
Injections

◆

Every year:
Take your rabbit to the vet centre for a check-up

Visiting your vet centre

The vets and nurses who work at your local vet centre want to help you keep your rabbit happy and healthy. They will tell you how to look after your rabbit properly. You can ask them as many questions as you like. The vet and nurse will also try to help make your rabbit better if it gets ill.

Small bandage

Large bandage

Strong carrying case

Salt sachets

Sticky tape

Scissors

Lint dressing

Disinfectant

Cotton wool

Nurse holds your rabbit for the vet

Listen with the stethoscope to hear your rabbit's heart

The first aid kit

Prepare a special first aid kit for your rabbit. The nurse will explain to you how to use everything. Just like you, your pet may graze or cut itself by accident. The kit contains all the things you will need to make it feel better on the way to the vet centre.

White coat keeps vet clean

Your vet's nurse
The nurse helps your vet. She knows a lot about rabbits. When you have any questions about your rabbit, visit or telephone the nurse at your vet centre.

Your vet
Your vet will give your rabbit special health checks. If your pet is ill, he will tell you what needs to be done to make it better. He may give you medicines for your pet.

My pet's fact sheet

Try making a fact sheet about your pet rabbit. Copy the headings on this page, or you can make up your own! Then write in the correct information about your rabbit.

White stripe
Brown back
Long brown ears
Fluffy tail
Twitching nose

Leave a space to stick in a photograph or draw a picture of your rabbit. Then label all of your pet's special features.

Name: **Tess**

Birthday: **28ᵗʰ September**

Weight: **2 Kg (4 ½ lb)**

Favourite fresh food: **Carrot**

Best game: **Hiding in a pipe**

Vet's name: **Mark Evans**

Nurse's name: **Rebecca Johns**

Vet centre telephone number: **089582 2324**

Injections

Your rabbit can pick up germs from wild animals when it is outside. To make sure it does not get ill, take it to your vet to have an injection every six months.

Index